D1291446

REVIEWS FOR
TALK YOURSELF INTO SUCCESS

"Susan's new book, *Talk Yourself Into Success*, is insightful and powerful. Her experience as an athlete, mother and business-woman has given her the unique skill set to convert even the highest hurdles of adversity into surmountable speed bumps. I love her competitive fire and recommend this book to anyone who wants to elevate his or her level of confidence."

– Rick "Doc" Walker, former professional football player for the Washington Redskins and motivational speaker at Walker Corporate Consulting

"*Talk Yourself Into Success* is a new and unique take on how we can develop our ability to reflect on and understand our inner thoughts and feelings, and take positive action. Susan's approach to the current field of mindfulness is direct and easy to absorb given her refreshing examples and anecdotes that keep you reading and enjoying her clarity and directness. I could refer to any number of current books on mindfulness, yet for making positive changes and coming to a great understanding of ourselves, I think that Susan's book is a wonderful place to begin!"

– Dr. Lance Clawson, Psychiatrist

"As a hard-charging entrepreneur and executive, *Talk Yourself Into Success* is an excellent reminder of the power of the mind and how much it determines our outcomes in life. So many books are overly conceptual and do not provide readers with practical, clear takeaways or applicable actions steps. Not this one! What I liked most about the book was how Susan provided real stories and concrete action steps to go along with her self-talk strategies. Very refreshing and relatable content."

– Brandon Bal, CEO
Direct Source China

"*Talk Yourself Into Success* is a solidly written, self-help guide to achieving and maintaining a positive state of mind. The author shares many of her own experiences ... thus giving the reader specific and practical tips on how to develop and keep daily habits that will have a positive effect on your life. It's chock full of many concrete examples on how to rid yourself of negative thoughts that block your success. It's an easy, worthwhile read. Enjoy!"

– Sheila Rogovin, Ph. D.

"As I read Susan Commander Samakow's new book, *Talk Yourself Into Success*, I found myself nodding and thinking, 'Not only is she courageous, she is right!' Beautifully written and filled with practical suggestions and exercises, Susan challenges us to be more awake and fulfilled each day. Reading the book is a lot like having a personal coach by your side asking insightful questions and cheering you on. This is a great book for members of a book club to discuss."

– Joan Wangler, M.Ed., M.S., ICF Master Certified Coach

"*Talk Yourself Into Success* is a step-by-step guide to self-awareness and positive growth. Through the author's personal struggles and self-evaluation, she has developed a framework of clear strategies and attainable solutions for living with strength, empowerment and healthy attitude. An important read for all who will challenge themselves to make positive change."

– Dr. Tobie Beckerman, M.D.
Beckerman's Women's Health

"*Talk Yourself Into Success* is a must read for anyone who wants to take back the reigns of power for steering the direction of their life. As a divorced woman I was moved by Susan's grasp of propelling oneself out of divorce successfully. Her strategies are essential tools for making your best life possible through life's challenges. This read helps you realize your success lies within yourself, and you are the only one waiting to unleash it's potential."

– Taryn Hoffman, Executive Director
Green Side Up Foundation

"Susan has mastered the art of ask, believe, and receive. Her message is one of hope, and that you are not a product of the things that have happened to you; but rather of what you are able to become as a result of your experiences. *Talk Yourself Into Success* is a guide that helped me to see the real beauty in me, the real beauty in the universe and how we are all connected, and how it can all be applied to our personal and professional lives. Susan shares personal experiences, which engages the reader to the author, and helps you towards achieving ultimate success in life, love, and business."

– Dr. Sarah Cassou, DC, Business Director

"Susan has powerfully and simply shared a blueprint that allows you to live a life of ease and resilience. This book will touch your heart and support you moving forward with inspired action."

– Rivka From, Personal & Executive Coach

"If you're looking to change the way you think about your life and ways to be happier, and you are struggling with where to start and how to see it through, then read *Talk Yourself Into Success*! It is a step-by-step guide to disentangling your negative thoughts and beliefs and instead focusing on creating positive thoughts by choice, after all, being happy is a choice. Filled with exercises and instructions, this book is a true roadmap to living a happy life. Highly recommend!"

– Abigail Bensimhon, Banker

"Susan book, *Talk Yourself Into Success*, is an easy read, full of useful strategies that expand the reader's ability to make sense of life's issues that we all must confront. It is insightful and simple in its application to everyday concerns that always pop-up. Susan's book gives you techniques that help you navigate your day. I recommend the book to everyone!"

– Ron Ogens, Attorney
Offit Kurman Attorneys at Law

"Susan's book, *Talk Yourself Into Success*, shares the importance that our internal messages plays in creating stories throughout our lives. With her practical insights, wisdom and personal experiences, positive self-talk strategies will help guide you to increase resiliency, results and move toward positivity – it is a must read in today's often cynical and critical world."

– Wendy S. Swire, Author, Speaker and Thought Leader
Co-author, Anytime Coaching

"Reading *Talk Yourself Into Success* opened my eyes to the possibility of changing old ingrained habits. With Susan's tools and guidelines you can break negative cycles and lead a more productive and healthy life."

– Greg Wheaton, Director of Tennis
USPTA Professional

TALK YOURSELF
into
SUCCESS

TALK YOURSELF
into
SUCCESS

STRATEGIES FOR
POSITIVE SELF-TALK,
CONFIDENCE AND
RESILIENCE

SUSAN COMMANDER SAMAKOW, PCC, CPCC

ACKNOWLEDGEMENTS

With gratitude and appreciation I want to thank you all for providing me with love, support, and inspiration.

To the loves of my life, Ashley and Courtney, we share a bond that gets stronger through time. You inspire me daily. You are in my heart and soul.

To Rivvy, who has been my special angel through my journey. Your love, guidance, and support is immeasurable. Thank you for lighting my path!

To Ellie, my wonderful editor, whose suggestions were appreciated, and whose friendship I value.

To Paul, who encouraged me to write, write, write … and is my in-house editor. Your love and support are never taken for granted. I'm still drumming away!

To Ma, Da & Grandma, who I hold in my heart and soul each and every day.

To all who reviewed my book, thank you for gracious comments and your time.

SPECIAL ACKNOWLEDGEMENT

The late Dr. Wayne Dyer was my entry point into self-talk and he encouraged me to continue on my path. Thank you for your words of wisdom. It was because of you that I became the Self-Talk Coach.

If you believe it will work out, you'll see opportunities.
If you believe it won't, you will see obstacles.
– WD

TABLE OF CONTENTS

MY STORY – TIES THAT BIND

*Do not underestimate the Power of Thoughts. Just as water has
the power to shift and mold Earth's landscape, your thoughts
have the power to shift and mold the landscape of your life.*
– Chuck Danes

We are what we think and what we make ourselves. This is my story, one that kept going back to using positive self-talk and being resilient, even before I really knew what each of those meant. My story is a lifetime of examples of thinking positively and being able to respond to situations in a productive way. It is my journey, which is still in progress, and for which I am grateful because I now understand these concepts. As a person and as a professional certified coach, I use these concepts for myself and for many others. I hope you find my story and this book empowering, so you too can have a healthy, productive, and satisfying life.

I share my story with you because as the story goes, I was able to take lemons and make lemonade. If you want a life greater than it is right now, read on. Whether you view my story as ordinary or extraordinary, use it to further yourself. I know you can.

~

Everyone has a story. That story can define your life. Everyone's story will change as life progresses. Know that you can create new life stories, the ones you want, as you learn and experience life.

You can be as positive as you want using select strategies to make things happen. To paraphrase Tony Robbins, *You're not going to go to the west and see the sun rise no matter how positive you are. You need a strategy to accomplish what you want.* I have the strategies for you to do so.

~

Man plans and G-d laughs.
— Yiddish Proverb

Follow me as I wind through my past. I have interjected some "present-day" thoughts as I found them relevant to my past.

MY EARLY AND FORMATIVE YEARS

The first thing I remember that happened in my life that significantly influenced me took place when I was five years old. My grandfather passed away, and my grandma Ada moved in with us, in Brooklyn, New York. Her moving was a life changing moment for me. It influenced and shaped my life personally and professionally.

Before my grandma moved in, my brother and I had separate rooms. That changed. We ended up sharing a room so that my grandmother could have her own space. She lived with us for five years, until I was ten. These are very influential years in anyone's life.

I took many positive lessons from my grandmother. There were also a few beliefs from her not-so-positive perspective that left significant impacts upon me.

I remember her saying to me that the "black cloud" was following us. I would literally look up in the sky for the black cloud. I knew by the tone in her voice that it was not something good. You could feel the doom and gloom.

Another "grandma-ism" that stuck with me was, *If you laugh in the morning you will cry at night.* Can you imagine? Yet, this was her belief system. And although I was a child, there was something within me telling me that notion was not true. I can close my eyes at any time and literally hear my grandma saying these things.

In fact, I recently asked my brother if these things were said to him. I asked him if she told him he had to stop doing something he liked, such as playing an instrument or sports. He had no idea what I was saying. It was then when I really understood how two children growing up in the same home could have such different experiences.

I remember sitting quietly, comparing my thoughts with those of my grandma's, and "listening" to what I now know was my gut intuition. I am an observer and a questioner. These qualities are fed by an awareness of my feelings and thoughts.

> ***Present-day thinking.*** Listening to your gut in today's world is hard. What I believe makes it hard is that we have busy, hectic lives, and we are surrounded by atten-tion-demanding technology, external noise, and internal chatter, or self-talk, all of which prevent having a "quiet

time" that is needed. We all will miss that opportunity to focus, unless we make a conscious effort to give ourselves that time.

Many of us miss signals and signs that we are exposed to every day from the universe. We miss them because there are endless distractions. Unless we carve out some quiet time we do not give ourselves the opportunity to receive significant messages that are there for us.

For example, I started noticing more signs when I deepened my self-awareness and learned more about how we are sent these messages. I would ask my grandmother to 'visit me,' whether in dreams or during the day. I was once sitting in front of the computer and I really wanted to connect with my grandmother, or my father, when the number 213 went across my screen. My grandmother's birthday was February 13th. I have had similar signals; they make me feel like I am being watched over by angels.

As more and more people are choosing a lifestyle change, looking for a better quality of life than just work, work, work, taking a time-out in their lives is a must. Many people are on a continuous "chase and conquer" path. In other words, set a goal, accomplish it, and move on to the next. Repeat, rinse, repeat! I urge you to take a few minutes and internalize your accomplishments no matter how big or small. I believe time-outs are regularly needed.

~

I remember when my girls were younger and I was single parenting, I would occasionally tell them that I was taking a ten-minute time-out. That short break really helped.

There are a growing number of people practicing mindfulness, yoga, taking pauses through each day with breath work, or just taking a step back and giving themselves a "quiet-time." Sometimes we just need a reminder. I tell my clients that I am their voice of interruption, to remind them to take a breather when needed.

~

Not too long after my grandmother moved in, my mother began to work outside the home. Two women do not normally run a single household, and my grandmother was not ready to work outside the home. So it was grandma Ada who was there when we came home for lunch and after school. Talk about having a change of influence!

I knew from my mother what a hard life my grandmother had. Her natural default had her look at life from a fearful, negative perspective. She also suffered from depression after her best friend, my grandpa Irving, died. Back then (1960's) they didn't have the knowledge and resources that exist today to deal with depression, and then, depression had a negative stigma.

Present-day thinking. Depression is now more widely understood and accepted, as are many other conditions. If you break your leg you wear a cast. If you scrape your arm, you clean it up. If you have depression you get help – counseling, and sometimes medicine. My philosophy is you do the best you can to take care of yourself and make healthy decisions.

I look at depression like a fence with a missing link. With the help of medication and behavioral change, you can fill in that missing link and continue to move forward successfully instead of continuing with a disconnect.

~

At an early age I loved sports and music. My grandmother, unfortunately, did not believe girls should play sports or certain musical instruments.

My brother, Scott, was four years older than I was. I idolized him. Everything he did I wanted to do. He played every sport and I wanted to follow him. I was a natural athlete, so sports came to me easily, and they still do. Sports and music serve as a wonderful way to reduce stresses in my life.

The first time I went to play ball in the New York schoolyard I got into trouble with my grandmother. She found out that I played and told me that girls do not play sports, that sports were not lady-like. That night my mother reiterated my grandmother's words. Why she and my father went along I do not know. I could not understand what a sport or musical instrument had to do with a person's gender.

Being athletic by nature, I was the girl who was chosen to play sports with the boys. Here is how I managed to be part of the team. Looking back, it was a Herculean effort by a little kid.

The schoolyard was three blocks from our apartment and a boy would be posted at each of the corners to let me know when my grandmother was coming so that I did not get caught.

It is not that my grandmother actively tried to stop me from doing the things I loved. She viewed things very differently. The term 'tomboy' was used widely and had a negative connotation. Thank goodness those concepts have changed and continue to improve.

My grandmother wanted to stop me from many things that I was good at and that I enjoyed. That was one of the first times I remember thinking to myself, *I'm not going to stop playing. I'm not doing anything wrong.* I did not let my grandmother's perspective stop me where I had a choice.

It is hard for a child to advocate for herself. I know I was upset at the time. I managed to play sports and play instruments, but not in a "carefree" way. When you are concerned about doing something that you are not supposed to be doing, engaging in whatever that is does not allow for either a free nor an easy feeling.

Present-day thinking. Sports are a great opportunity to gain confidence. You will win or lose, and learn that it is totally acceptable to lose. When we learn this concept early enough we learn that there is nothing wrong with failing or losing. Hopefully we learn how to accept results gracefully. It helps prepare us for other challenges we will face in our lives.

Sports can also teach us resiliency. If we lose a game we can learn to focus on the failure and to get up and go on, bigger, better, faster or smarter next time. We can learn that a loss today can mean we can play better the next time.

The other "no" directed by grandma was that playing certain musical instruments was also not feminine. At the time my school offered a music program that included a student choosing an instrument and receiving group lessons. It was a great opportunity.

I really liked the clarinet. My female cousin played and I thought it was cool. I played for three weeks and was doing well, and enjoying it. Then my mother told me that I had to stop playing because my grandmother said *blowing instruments was not feminine.* I ended up playing piano for years (which I did not mind, but it was not my first choice). Thank goodness I did not tell them that my real desire was to play the drums! Can you imagine what the reaction would have been? So guess what?

As an adult, my husband (I remarried in 1996) gave me a drum set and lessons as a gift! I really enjoy banging and drumming away. It was one of the most thoughtful gifts I ever received and a great stress reducer!

Present-day thinking. Of course my grandmother was not trying to purposely scare me. This was how she viewed life and it greatly influenced our household. As it is with most people, we view things from our own perspective, or lens, and that is how we see the world. What is important is to recognize that when we view things we all have our own biases that color what we see.

I believe my grandma and parents did the best they could. In fact, my mother said my grandmother did the same things to her. Why my mother continued that, well that is something that would be her story to tell.

Looking back I feel sad that my grandmother actually believed there was a "black cloud" hanging over us. She was a loving, warm, and intelligent person. There was a lot that I gained from her and I always felt her giving from her heart. I still talk to her all the time. I know she is listening.

What I did not know at the time was that much of my life's work would center on self-talk.

We all make choices. We decide how to frame a situation. Choose to be productive and you will thrive.

My grandma's directives had me focus on self-talk.

Self-talk has an incredible positive and negative impact on everyone's life. What can be more important than what we are saying to ourselves since it impacts us mentally, physically, spiritually, and energetically? The mind-body connection is literally that strong.

When I was ten years old my family moved from New York to New Jersey. The commute back and forth every day soon got to be too much for my father. When we moved my grandmother decided to move out into her own place. She wanted to stay in New York. She was doing well and she was ready to be on her own. She had found her comfort zone.

> ***Present-day thinking.*** Back then people did not move as freely as they do today. Moving to another state was like moving to another country, and from everything I know about transitions and changes, even when they are positive, most of us are "hardwired" to resist. It is hard for people to leave their comfort zone. That is why I urge people to take baby steps in a forward direction as opposed to a grand leap. I find when people try to take the grand leap they end up smacking into the wall and getting stuck. Taking forward-moving baby steps keeps them moving towards what they desire.

$\sim$

My high-school years were good. Thank goodness for sports. I developed wonderful friendships, survived the normal up's and down's of those years (positive self-talk and resiliency all the while working and me not fully realizing how powerful these tools were), and then, on to college. My brother went to the University of Maryland, in College Park, Maryland. I visited him and fell in love with the school and campus. So there I went and after graduation, I chose to stay in the Washington, D.C. metropolitan area, and I continue to live there today.

Fast-forward side-note. I am happy to share that my daughters played the instruments and sports they chose. What is important is that I knew that my story, that is my grandmother denying me sports and music activity, would not be my daughters' story.

CONTINUING MY STORY INTO ADULTHOOD

After college I decided to stay in Maryland. I had a few jobs, and I got married. I had my girls. I thought I had a great life. Slowly I saw my marriage dissolving.

At 35, I decided that if nothing changed within the next year, despite doing everything I could to keep the marriage together, I would file for divorce. It sadly ended.

My girls were 7 and 3-1/2 at the time. I knew in many ways I would have an uphill battle, and I did. I wanted sole custody. I got it. The child support I briefly received did not fill a cavity, and alimony, well, that was a joke.

On my own, I applied for and won a $5,000 grant from a social services agency. With that money I bought a computer and took two computer classes to make myself job-ready. The girls would soon be in school full-days. In the late 80's and early 90's a single woman working outside the home was not as common as it is today.

Early mornings were a hard time of the day for me. It took a lot of energy to get going. My girls and my drive to succeed were my motivation. I was their advocate. I was on a mission. I was building a career.

I recognized I needed help. While my parents and friends were very supportive, I also sought out and found other women in the same situation, so I would have a support group.

My sister-in-law gave me a copy of Dr. Seuss's book *Oh the Places You'll Go* and then a friend gave me *The Little Engine That Could* by Wally Piper. I kept those books on my desk as I worked (and they are still on my desk). They are what I call positive structures ... something positive that I could hold onto that motivated and inspired me.

My parents would come to visit from New Jersey once a month and stay for the weekend. They were a real source of stability for the girls and me. We were blessed.

I would also drive to see my parents in New Jersey. Playing Taylor Dayne's *Love Will Lead You Back* CD motivated me. Divorced, I learned first hand the power of resiliency.

When I was going through my divorce I really noticed my self-talk. During times of transition our self-talk gets louder and faster, and mine was screaming at me!

My divorce produced tough times, but my perseverance, and my survivor mode kicked in. From the moment I decided to pursue my divorce, I have never looked back with regret, not even for a moment.

It was during my divorce process that I developed my positive self-talk strategies. These are proven strategies that helped and continue to support clients shift from nonproductive, negative self-talk to productive, positive self-talk. I was moving forward and creating a life that would work for my girls and for me.

> ***Present-day thinking***. I teach that to make changes,
> you have to be aware. In order to become more aware,
> you have to develop your "awareness muscle." It takes
> awareness, practice, and commitment. You are develop-
> ing a new pattern and you have to be consistent and
> habitual ... that is why I am repeating this here (and I
> will again later in this book), so you begin to deepen
> your awareness.

Awareness, practice, commitment = new habit!

One example I used to create more awareness for myself was with sticky notes. I wrote the letter "A" for "awareness" on the smallest size sticky notes. I posted them everywhere: on my computer, in my desk drawer, the mirror, the refrigerator, by my toothbrush ... you get the picture. Had I known all the sticky notes I was going to use I would have invested in 3M stock!

And by the way, did I mention it is good to keep your sense of humor no matter what is going on?

Where I saw roadblocks, I chose to view them as options. I did not let naysayers stop me. Choice is empowering. I believe that is how I have persevered through life ... through positive self-talk, choice, viewing things through different perspectives, focusing on what I have instead of what is missing, and having a resilient mindset.

I do not believe I did anything special or anything that anyone else cannot do. I noticed. I was aware. I was committed to learning and moving forward in the different aspects of my life. I asked myself, *How did I get here?* The answer is a simple one: choice by choice by choice. I take responsibility for those choices. If something does not work out, I do not blame others. Blaming keeps you stuck and prevents you from the necessary taking of responsibility for your actions or words.

~

My coaching career began before coaching was a career. I developed three home-based jobs before working from home was "the norm." To say the very least, I was scared, actually terrified! I was so worried about the "what if's." My mother told me to take one day at a time, which became one of my mantras. The other mantra I learned was, no matter what, I'll manage. It was from a wonderful therapist who saw my ex-husband and me for a blink of time.

I still keep the piece of paper that I originally wrote that phrase on in my dresser drawer.

As I mentioned, I began coaching before it was a recognized occupation. I was "coaching" people in the areas of business, life, career, leadership, and relationships. I found my life's passion and calling as a coach. I also had many clients that were stressed and I began teaching them breathing exercises, meditation, mindfulness, and Emotional Freedom Technique (EFT) or tapping. I thought what could I teach to clients that is healthy for them and me ... it is a win-win!

I watched the field for several years to make sure coaching was not a fad. I was very careful how I spent my time and money. When I saw the field was here to stay I enrolled in coaching school and was soon certified by the school and the International Coach Federation. If I was going to make this my career then I was going to do it the right way and get the appropriate schooling and training.

Coaching came naturally to me and I have been successful doing it. I often compare sports coaching to business and life coaching. You are there to guide and support people but not to do things for them. I provided the tools so clients can manage their lives.

Like the saying goes, *Give a man a fish, and you feed him for a day. Teach a man to fish, and you feed him for a lifetime.*

My coaching skills came from my athletic background. I could help a client write a plan, set goals and provide accountability, and understand and thus coach the player, or in this case, the client, that he or she had to take the ball and run.

> ***Present-day thinking***. My game plan has always been that if you fall down you pick yourself up and learn from successes and failures. Do your best and use your personal or core values to reach your goals.
>
> Be in integrity with yourself. In other words, have your actions and words match! Take a step outside your comfort zone, even if it is a little scary. Focus and move forward toward being energized and away from being depleted.

That is what I have done and continue to do. I support and guide people to reach their goals, provide account-ability, and motivate and inspire clients. Everything I did was coaching. It allowed me to stay in a productive, positive, and resilient mindset.

And once the storm is over, you won't remember how you made it through, how you managed to survive. You won't even be sure, whether the storm is really over. But one thing is certain. When you come out of the storm, you won't be the same person who walked in. That's what this storm's all about.
— Haruki Murakami

MY FORMULA FOR YOU

WAKE UP EXCITED AND GO TO SLEEP FULFILLED

How good would it feel to wake up in the morning and have a strong start to the day? Then, even better, at the end of the day, to be able to say I woke up excited and went to sleep fulfilled!

I did not always wake up excited or go to sleep feeling fulfilled. Twenty something years ago when I was going through separation, divorce, and getting back into the job market my self-talk was very future-oriented. When I woke up in the morning I was full of "what if's." I would say, *What if this happens? What if that happens?* It was very scary. Having a lot of "what ifs" creates anxiety and does not feel good.

Even as I sit here writing this I can close my eyes and put myself back in those moments. I can remember that queasy feeling in my stomach. With the knowledge I have now, I am able to shift and reframe those thoughts and feelings in my body to something positive. What I know now is not to be afraid of my feelings and not to sweep them away. It is okay to feel uncomfortable. We have a tendency to want to push away uncomfortable feelings, and when we do, they never really go away. That is why I recommend these three steps if you are avoiding something or uncomfortable:

1. Notice how you feel.

2. Experience the feeling instead of trying to push it away.

3. Take a productive step; even a baby step is productive.

~

During my divorce process I realized I needed something positive to hold onto, something that would not cost anything, some type of positive structure. That is when I began to develop my positive self-talk strategies. I use them daily and have successfully used them with hundreds of clients, friends, and relatives.

Simply put, my strategies work. I am proof of that. If they help me, they can help you!

My positive self-talk strategies, combined with resilience techniques (some of which I learned from the ideas Karen Revich and Andrew Shatte share in their book *The Resilience Factor*) can guide you to having a productive life. There is no magic pill. There is, however, a formula that works for me, and the hundreds of people I have coached.

THE FORMULA IS A SIMPLE ONE:

Productive and Positive Self-Talk (Part 1)

+

Resilience (Part 2)

=

Thriving, Flourishing Life (Part 3)

Glinda, the Good Witch in *The Wizard of Oz*, tells Dorothy: *You always had the power my dear, you just had to learn it for yourself.*

Dorothy: *Oh, will you help me? Can you help me?*

Glinda: *You don't need to be helped any longer. You've always had the power to go back to Kansas.*

Dorothy: *I have?*

Scarecrow: *Then why didn't you tell her before?*

Glinda: *She wouldn't have believed me. She had to learn it for herself.*

Scarecrow: *What have you learned, Dorothy?*

Dorothy: *Well, I—I think that it, that it wasn't enough just to want to see Uncle Henry and Auntie Em — and it's that — if I ever go looking for my heart's desire again, I won't look any further than my own backyard. Because if it isn't there, I never really lost it to begin with! Is that right?*

Glinda: *That's all it is!*

Scarecrow: *But that's so easy! I should've thought of it for you.*

Tin Man: *I should have felt it in my heart.*

Glinda: *No, she had to find it out for herself. Now those magic slippers will take you home in two seconds!*

Dorothy: *Oh! Toto too?*

Glinda: *Toto too.*

Dorothy: *Now?*

Glinda: *Whenever you wish.*

Glinda: *Then close your eyes and tap your heels together three times. And think to yourself "There's no place like home."*

No matter what is going on in your life, every aspect of it is impacted by your self-talk. Focus on what you are saying to yourself. What you say to yourself, what you think, is what happens in your life. It impacts the relationships you are in, the careers you choose, and the self-imposed limits you put on yourself. Choice by choice by choice, we create our lives. So what are you saying to yourself? What are the choices that you are making? We are each responsible for the choices we make.

~

FINDING "THE DAVID" WITHIN US

As the story goes, Michelangelo was given a huge slab of granite, and he was asked to create something. After working on it every day, almost every hour, for months, he created a magnificent sculpture known as "David."

Consider two perspectives of the story. First, Michelangelo chipped away at the stone and created, formed and molded David. The other perspective is that David was always in there and Michelangelo had to chip away at the excess stone, the clutter, or what I call negative self-talk, to get to the final beautiful form.

I believe David is within all of us. We are all MAGNIFICENT! We just sometimes have to chip away at the layers, the outside sources and influences that have us looking at ourselves with limited thoughts. The better alternative is to look at ourselves as being unlimited, with unused potential. We all have that! Unleash your magnificence. See David within you and within the people in your relationships.

~

Let's look at getting to a productive life. I said there are three parts to this formula. It is not complicated, but stay with me.

I. FORMULA PART ONE

PRODUCTIVE, POSITIVE SELF-TALK

*I think we all have a little voice inside us that will guide us
... if we shut out all the noise and clutter from our lives and
listen to that voice it will tell us the right thing to do.*
– Christopher Reeve

What is Self-Talk?

Self-talk is our inner dialogue, our thoughts, our chatter, or what I call our internal board of directors. It runs like a ticker tape from the minute we get up in the morning until we go to sleep at night. Even when we are sleeping our subconscious is busy at work.

Our self-talk determines the limits we set for ourselves and colors how we view things. Our self-talk can control us with self-imposed limits or it can free us by thoughts of options and possibilities. What we think is what becomes our reality. And perception is reality!

WHY IS SELF-TALK SO IMPORTANT?

Self-talk is the determining factor for how we live our lives. We live our lives based on our thoughts. We make our decisions and judgments based on our thoughts. What we say, what we think, and what we do influences our actions, reactions, behaviors and attitudes about life. Our thoughts impact the relationships we are in and the careers we choose.

Coming from a positive, productive mindset is the best alternative, because, again, what you think is what happens in your life.

WHERE DOES SELF-TALK COME FROM?

Our self-talk began at an early age, literally as soon as we began thinking. As children we were greatly influenced by the adults in our lives - parents, teachers, and religious figures. And although some of the things that were said to us were not meant to be criticisms, they might have negatively impacted us. They are things like ... you are not good enough, fast enough, smart enough, thin enough. Over time individuals internalized these comments and take them to mean "I'm not enough." As kids we took on what was said to us as if it were fact, or the only truth, or set in stone. Without realizing it, many of us took this mindset into adulthood.

We have one hundred positive thoughts and one negative thought, and guess what? We focus on the one negative! We play it over and over like a tape.

I say change the tape! Stop reinforcing the negative. How? By rewiring the brain ... by creating new neural pathways.

Understanding how the brain works is helpful, so here is a bit of the science, in lay terms, behind the thoughts.

A BRIEF OVERVIEW: THE BRAIN: HOW DO YOU CHANGE THE TAPE?

Thanks to the latest brain research, we now know we can rewire our brain at any stage of life. Yes, at any age. This is called neuroplasticity.

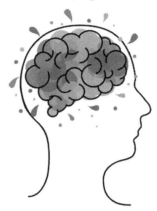

Changing the tape is a combination of changing our thoughts and creating new neural pathways. Our brains <u>can</u> be rewired.

Think of a neural pathway as a river and our thoughts as the water. When the water continues in the same path it creates and defines the river's depth, and width. Similarly, the more we think a certain way, the repetition of those thoughts, be they negative or positive, the more the brain's pathways are defined and deepened.

New thoughts create new neural pathways. If we keep thinking a certain way it deepens that new neural pathway and becomes our new "normal," or a new habit, while the old negative pathway fades out because those old negative thoughts are no longer traveling down the river.

Here is an example: Think of when you were learning to drive a car. Everything you did was a conscious thought. First you put the key in the ignition. Next you adjusted the seat and the mirrors. You shifted the car gears from park, to reverse or drive, then you looked both ways before you pulled out. You were very aware of the different steps you needed to take to drive the car.

After repeating this day after day, you created a new habit so that after several days or weeks when you went to the car to drive, you did those steps automatically. That became your new pattern. The new neural pathways were now being used.

Think of a time when you had a disagreement with someone. Did you replay the disagreement over and over in your head? Each time you think about the disagreement with someone, your brain took it in like it was new. It was taking it in as "disagreement ... disagreement ... disagreement"; as if you had several disagreements instead of only one.

Want to understand this on a deeper level?

Your brain cannot distinguish between what is fact and what is imagined. Think about that for a moment. Your brain does not know what is real; it just registers "presence," and you, by default, perceive what is there as being real. If you make a mistake and keep thinking about it, your brain is taking it in like "mistake ... mistake ... mistake."

The point is, simply, your thoughts affect you. Why not have positive, productive thoughts? People sooner believe that if something negative happens something else negative will happen. This is not the case as much with the positive. Many people do not see positive leading to more positive. Do not buy into the "waiting for the other shoe to drop" mentality. Take control of your thoughts and reframe anything not productive into the productive.

The next time you make a mistake or have a disagreement, afterwards, notice how many times you thought about the incident. One time? Three times? Ten times? Can you now retrain yourself to stop thinking about it so it is not deepening a neural pathway with negative thoughts? Reframe the negative to positive ... use your time productively.

~

UNDERSTANDING THE BRAIN ALLOWS US TO MAKE CHANGES

According to The National Science Foundation we have approximately 50,000 thoughts each day and about 77% of them are negative. I thought that 77% was too high a percentage, so I checked it out for myself and found it to be true. Positive thoughts are like a fleeting moment. They last approximately 20 seconds while negative thoughts multiply by the thousands, neuron by neuron.

Early man's primitive brain was wired for survival and protection. If not, then back in the caveman days, when the caveman left the cave he would have been eaten by a tiger. We want to retrain our caveman brain.

~

FIGHT, FLIGHT OR FREEZE

At our brain's most primitive, or reptilian level, the autonomic nervous system takes over.

The reptilian brain in us functions like a gas pedal in a car. When stressed or scared, it triggers the fight, flight or freeze response, providing the body with a burst of hormones so that it can respond to perceived threats or dangers. We call this response stress.

So you will know, when we get stressed or triggered, a tiny part in our brain, the size of a lima bean, called the amygdala (part of the limbic system), signals the FFF response to protect us (called amygdala hijacking). Stress hormones - cortisol, adrenaline, and norepinephrine - are automatically released into our bodies.

Stress puts us into the FFF response mode. Repeated stress ends up taking a toll on our immune system.

When we are in the FFF mode, or when we are stressed, it is not a good time to make decisions. Stress and fear-based decisions do not typically work out the way we would want.

When was the last time you made a fear-based decision? What was the outcome?

~

Stress depletes us. When our self-talk is fear or stress-based it is not positive. We go in a direction that is unproductive. The impact that has on us is that we shut down.We are resistant. Our creativity is blocked. Our trust is low. We come from a place of being "I" centric instead of "we" centric. Thus, if collaboration or co-creating is a possible better outcome, we will not get there. When our resilience is low, our self-talk is negative, and our conversations tend to be unhealthy.

What can you do to down-regulate the negative and up-regulate the positive?

When we shift our thinking from the primitive or reptilian part of the brain (located in the base of the back of the head) to the pre-frontal cortex (above the forehead) part of the brain, the hormones oxytocin and dopamine (the "feel good" hormones) are released and we are able to be more open, creative, and trusting. Our resilience is higher. We have more positive self-talk, and we have more healthy reactions and conversations.

Shifting thoughts to the positive creates new neural pathways. The good news is that the shifting, the rewiring of our brain, can take place at any stage of life even if we have been thinking negatively for years!

My positive self-talk strategies will help you shift. In addition, breathing techniques like taking a breath, holding the breath for at least six seconds, and then releasing the breath (and you can repeat) are helpful in calming ourselves down.

II. FORMULA PART TWO

RESILIENCE

Many people think resilience is bouncing back. It is, but it is much more than that!

Resilience is a thinking style and guides how we deal with adversity in our lives. In other words, how we think about situations or people either energizes us or depletes us. The mindset we have shapes how we see things and determines our energy level. If our energy is depleted or heading in that direction, then our resilience level will be lower.

Think of resilience as a muscle we have to build, like a muscle in our arm. The more we work out, the stronger the arm becomes. The same is true of resilience. The more we practice our reactions to adversity, the more resilient we become.

If you are resilient, you can look at situations differently. For instance, when you have adversity in your life, do you see a stepping-stone or an obstacle? Do you see hardships or challenges? How do you view failure? How do you feel when things do not go the way you want?

Resiliency adopts a healthy, productive attitude. When looking at resilience in a productive, positive way we have the mindset to see situations as stepping-stones, not obstacles, and as challenges, not hardships.

Failure is something from which we can learn. It is not the opposite of success but rather an integral part of success. I want to emphasize that it is how we *react* to situations that will determine how resilient we are. How we react is a choice. Look at setbacks as opportunities that can energize us. Max Planck, a German physicist who was the father of quantum theory once said, *When you change the way you look at things, the things you look at change.* Nothing has to change except our perspectives.

When I was going through separation and divorce, it felt like a roller coaster ride. There were many ups and downs. I steadily built my resilience by taking forward-moving baby steps. I did not realize at the time I was actually building it. I was on automatic pilot and thinking survival, which when looking back took resilience. My divorce process reminded me of the Olympic swimmers. I noticed how the swimmers would glance to the left and right to see where their competition was, and then how they turned back to look straight ahead and stay focused.

I learned that when I was really upset, my energy levels sank. I became depleted. I had to learn not to let negative situations drain me. The less time spent in the depleting mode, the better off I was. I soon came to realize there would be good days and bad days and that I needed to take good care of myself. I began to talk to myself saying that the negative emotions were not going to get me anywhere but down the rabbit hole.

I came to learn that no matter how frustrating the situation, I had to turn it into a constructive opportunity. I would ask myself, *Is being angry going to help me or hurt me?* How did I want to fill my time, with unproductive, negative thoughts or productive, positive thoughts? Sometimes, if that process did not get me over the hurdle, I would do something physical like working out on my step machine. There were days when I stepped enough to reach the top of Mt. Everest.

Life ends up being about the decisions and choices we make. If I make a bad decision, I look at how I can remedy the situation. The more experiences I have like that, the more I get to practice and the better the outcome in a shorter amount of time. Practicing resilience has helped me to successfully deal with adversity and how to make a decision, trust my gut, and move on. That has become my new normal and it feels good. It feels right. It will for you too!

~

Stress often comes, unfortunately, from situations that arise and interactions we have with other people. I developed a resilience process for those times. My process to eliminate those types of situations is fairly simple. First, I require that people deal with me honestly and respectfully. If they cannot, and there is no willingness to try to honor those values, the conversation is over.

If the conversation continues, desirably of course, what I then look to do is to understand issues that are prohibiting the success of the situation, develop strategies to ensure success, and be helpful with the resolution of the underlying conflict.

Like many people, I encounter tough situations. I view these as gifts allowing me to keep learning and strengthening my reactions so they are healthy, and resilient reactions. The universe is giving me the opportunity to keep practicing. Over the years I have had plenty of practice and wanted a constructive way of dealing with stressful situations. I learned here on "Earth school" that I might as well get it right and learn it now, or the universe will keep providing me with situations from which to learn.

When there is an adverse situation, I often take a pause and give it some thought. I ask myself, what can I do to turn things around? How can I handle things differently so I reach a better outcome? I also ask myself, *Did my decision come from a healthy, healed place?* That sort of thinking has me move from hurt to wholeness, and from an unhealed place to one that is healed. Doing this shifts things from unhealthy to healthy.

～

Positive self-talk and resilience are not innate. Anyone can master them by noticing or being aware of his or her thoughts, practicing healthy reactions and committing to not letting anything get in the way. Are some days better than others? Yes … and you have to give yourself permission to be human. We are not perfect. If you catch yourself in a negative thought, as soon as you realize it, shift or reframe your thinking or actions. That is being resilient! Instead of criticizing yourself that you blew it and did not catch yourself sooner with a negative thought, instead reframe to, *Okay, I'll catch myself sooner next time.* That is building your resilience and positive self-talk. There is no bigger bully in our lives than our own self-talk!

> *If you talk to others the way you talk to*
> *yourself would you be your friend?*
> — Rob Bremmer

Learn more: Resilience is further described in the book, *The Resilience Factor* by Karen Revich and Andrew Shatte.

III.   FORMULA PART THREE

THRIVING, FLOURISHING LIFE

What would it be like to wake up excited and go to sleep fulfilled? To me, that is a thriving, flourishing life when you feel satisfied and content with how your day has gone. You are ready to go to sleep and looking forward to waking up excited about the new day before you.

Each sunrise and sunset is a work of art. We have a clear canvas on how we are going to paint our day. If you are practicing positive self-talk, what are you saying to yourself? Are you resilient? Is your thinking style one that energizes you rather than depletes you? Are you moving in the direction of living a thriving, flourishing life? I say "yes" to all of these!

POSITIVE SELF-TALK STRATEGIES INTRODUCTION

I wrote my positive self-talk strategies when I was going through major transitions in my life ... separation, divorce and reentry into the job market. I use them personally and professionally.

My thirteen positive self-talk strategies will guide you, as they guide me every day, to a positive, productive, healthy life, as long as you are consistent with them. Treat learning the strategies as part of your daily ritual, and if you do not practice any rituals, now is a good time to start. Choose one or two strategies to focus on for one or two weeks and then keep moving forward. There is nothing difficult about them. Remember, you are forming new habits. This takes awareness, practice, and commitment.

Here is how I view rituals: they keep us connected. They ground us. They engage our hearts and get us out of our heads, which is where we spend most of our time.

If you want to live the life you were meant to live, this is a great place to start. You can live your life *on-purpose* and with intention, joy, positive energy, and emotion behind the effort of focusing your attention. If I did it, you can do it!

FOUR SELF-TALK QUESTIONS TO CONSIDER

1. Who has influenced your thinking about yourself, others, life, and success in general?

2. What are your beliefs, attitudes, habits, and thinking styles?

3. What societal attitudes, beliefs, and teachings are part of your mindset?

4. Do these thoughts attitudes, beliefs, and teachings enhance your success or limit it?

CHAPTER 1

Strategy 1 – Set Aside a Quiet Time

Our lives are so full of activity and chatter it's difficult to find quiet time … Those are the moments that are the most creative for me. The location is less important than the choice to turn other things off. Because I find that the quietest times of my life speak the loudest.
– Regina Dugan

Quiet the mind and the soul will speak.
– Unknown

We need quiet time to examine our lives openly and honestly – spending quiet time alone gives your mind an opportunity to renew itself and create order.
– Susan L. Taylor

There is nothing more important than starting your day with a Quiet Time (QT). This is your entry point into the day. You want to make it a good one.

QT can look many different ways. As the quotes above suggest, it does not matter where, but it is making the choice to take the time that is important. I cannot stress enough how important it is and strongly urge you to take a QT each morning. As your day progresses you will find other things believed to be "more important" and you will then rarely get back to taking that QT.

QT will help with focus, clarity, and navigation through each day.

Before you begin, by the way, seriously, before you start your QT, visit the bathroom. There is nothing that can be more disruptive than the need to make that visit.

Think about it: What is the first thing your body wants to do after a night of sleep? It wants that visit, so we get up and use the bathroom.

Your brain wants to do the same thing. It *needs* to release. We have so many thoughts, so much going on from day to day in our personal and professional lives that people *need* to clear out some of the thoughts in their head in order to allow more thoughts to enter. We *need* to clear the space to make more room. In order to clear the space you must first release. Quiet Time is the release for the brain.

WHAT DOES QUIET TIME LOOK LIKE?

What you do with your QT is up to you. A QT can look a lot of different ways. Some people meditate. Some think of their intentions for the day. Some do visualization. Some write in a gratitude journal. Some start with prayer. Take whatever time you have, whether it is ten minutes or thirty minutes to ground yourself. You want to feel like you are on solid or stable ground, like a tree that is rooted to the earth.

Set your intentions for the day and visualize what you would like your day to look like. "Seeing it" as if it were occurring is helpful. Many athletes use this technique. Golfers visualize the ball going in the hole before they take a stroke; when basketball players are at the foul line they see the swoosh before they shoot.

Do what works for you. It is not necessary to do everything every day because your time and needs are going to vary. Sometimes it depends on how much time you have. Make sure though to do something, even if it is for one minute, to acknowledge the QT, which will help ground you.

You can tell a QT has an impact if one day you skip it. I have had clients tell me that they simply feel "off" and I have experienced that same feeling when I was beginning the QT practice. At first I could not put my finger on it. I simply felt off; then I realized it was from skipping the grounding part of my day.

QT – OPPORTUNITY TO DE-CLUTTER

In the same way you de-clutter a closet, you can de-clutter your mind.

Think about the clothes that are in your closet. Is there anything that you have not worn in the past year? Is there anything that does not fit? Is there anything that still has the tags on it for the past year? Those items are taking up space in your closet. The clothes are clutter because they are serving no purpose. They are taking up a space that could be used for clothes you can wear.

De-clutter and get rid of those clothes. You can donate them, or bring them to a consignment shop. Release the space so you can fill it with other clothes, or maybe something else.

Many of us today have more than full plates. Many families have both parents working, or they are single-parent households. We have aging parents, or kids and grandkids we are responsible for, or issues at work, concerns about finances, errands to run, and multiple everyday stresses. Moreover, we are all multi-tasking even though our brains are wired to only do one thing at a time.

QT can help calm these stresses. I recommend getting anything that is not urgent off of your plate. Sometimes delegating helps. At the office, think of what you can delegate. Give kids some household responsibility … everyone has to work together. My advice, try not to overburden kids. They too have many responsibilities and concerns: school, activities, and social status. Some kids are building the "college" resumes when they are in middle school. Yes, there is a great deal of pressure on all of us.

QT – RELEASE AND WRITE DOWN

During QT your mind will wander and perhaps plan. Once your mind is cleared, it allows for planning. How is your memory? Not everything that rushes through during QT may be remembered.

One simple way to remember is to write things down. When I think of something, I email myself so that I do not forget. I also keep a small pad and pen on my night table because often I think of something in the middle of the night (so instead of hoping I will remember what it was in the morning, I jot it down). I have mastered writing in the dark! Once I do that I feel more relaxed to fall back asleep.

I am also a list maker. When I think of an item I need on a food list, I write it down. Then, of course, even if I forget to take the list to the store, simply having written it helps the memory process. I can close my eyes while I am shopping and think about what I wrote; then there is a good chance I will remember. If I do not remember anything, buying Ben & Jerry's *Coffee Buzz, Buzz, Buzz* always works!

Another advantage of recording thoughts onto paper or onto your smart phone is that the recording often spurs other ideas and thoughts.

When I have a workshop, I will write down the things I need to bring with me such as a laptop, a pad, tape, a flipchart, and so on.

In all these cases you are getting clutter out of your head and making space for new thoughts and ideas to enter.

To show you it works, practice this for several weeks and then stop for a day or two. You will really feel a difference in your day.

QT - GRATITUDE JOURNAL

During my QT, I think of three things for which I am grateful. I do this every morning and before I go to sleep in the evening. It is best to write what you are grateful for in a journal or a notebook, particularly if this is a new practice for you. You have a much greater chance of making this a habit by writing it down. For me, writing engrains my gratitude list in my memory. To make a new habit or pattern you have to be consistent and committed.

What is wonderful about this new habit of gratitude is that it is one of the highest energetic vibrations on the planet. A great source to learn more about this is David Hawkins' book, *Power versus Force*.

Gratitude, like everything, is energy. When you begin and end your day with gratitude, the energy created literally changes your brain at a cellular level. Of course you cannot see the energy, but think of radio waves coming from a tower. You cannot see them either, yet the radio waves produce sound that you hear from the waves' energy.

QT - SET YOUR INTENTIONS

The number one principle that rules my life is intention.
Thought by thought, choice by choice, we are co-creating
our lives based on the energy of our intention.
– Oprah Winfrey

Once I write in my gratitude journal, I sit back in bed or in a comfortable chair, close my eyes because it is less distracting, and think of how I would like my day to go. I ask myself, what do I want my day to look like? What do I want it to feel like? With both of these questions I picture myself going happily through the day, being as present as possible.

I then think about what my intentions are for the day or the week. Being mindful is focusing your attention on your intentions. In *The Power of Intention* by Dr. Wayne Dyer, he describes intention as, *Something that you can feel, connect with, know, and trust. It is an inner awareness that we explicitly feel.*

Some people focus intentions on what they want to accomplish or on what goals they want to reach. There is no right or wrong focus, or good or bad.

When I set my intentions for the day, I have direction, a way to center some of my thoughts. This allows me to organize myself, and my thoughts, and to think about how I am going to navigate through my day. Naturally there are days that are more stressful, but by being mindful, by being aware, I handle life in a calmer, more constructive way.

Also, realize that with each day there is the possibility that something will pull us off track. There are certainly too many emails to respond to, phone calls to return, and the never-ending putting out fires for a multitude of problems. We end up multi-tasking and touching on the surface of several things rather than focusing in on one or two items.

Plan some miscellaneous time so you are mentally prepared for the unexpected and acknowledge that events or people will pull you off track. That is a realistic certainty in a normal day's activities. This understanding reduces stress because you are then prepared. I visualize a compartment in my brain that prepares me to transition better from one activity to another with less stress.

QT - TIME FOR VISUALIZATION

A common tool for athletes, visualization is very effective in helping boost confidence, strength, and results. Most people think visualization is limited to what we see. Visualization can use all five senses, and using those senses is very effective. Certain smells and tastes can bring back memories.

I used visualization at different times in my life. I played basketball all through my school years. I would see the ball going swoosh through the hoop. In tennis, which I still play, I see me placing the ball out of reach of my opponent. In golf, I see the ball going into the hole before I even swing the club.

I faced a personal challenge when I was going through my coaching certification. Approximately six months before my coaching certification exam I began my visualization process.

I had several factors that were going on that were new to me. The testing was in northern California and it was the first time I was traveling alone. It was also the first time I was going to take both a written and oral exam, simultaneously.

When I took the exam, the process began with the written section. During the written section the test-taker was pulled out of the room to do the oral part of the exam. This process has since been changed because it was so disruptive.

The oral part was being videotaped. In the first coaching session an applicant coached one of the panel members, and in the second part the test-taker coached a colleague.

Each day I would see myself sitting in a room with a group of other coaches. Even though I did not know what the judges or my colleagues looked like, I pictured smiling faces. I heard laughter in the room, and I smelled fresh flowers. I also kept a postcard of a hot air balloon on my desk for the six months. I pictured myself and my husband going for a ride, in celebration of going through the process whether I passed or failed. For me it was celebratory no matter what the results.

I saw myself taking the test and being interrupted in the middle. All of this was helpful. What was amazing to me was that the day went along as I pictured. Because I visualized the interruption during the exam, it was not as disruptive as it could have been.

I have since used visualization many times and when the expected results come, it still feels like magic to me. It takes awareness, practice and commitment. Being consistent and habitual is key!

By the way, the hot air balloon ride was amazing!

SUGGESTIONS:

I have mentioned a few options for a QT. Choose what works for you whether it's one item or a few.

- Relieve or release yourself to make room for the things you do want in your life
- Think of your intentions for the day or week
- Visualize what you want
- Write in a gratitude journal

INQUIRY:

What are you willing to do to move closer to living the life you desire?

BOOK SUGGESTION:

Power of Intention by Dr. Wayne Dyer

CHAPTER 2

Strategy #2 – Be Aware, Be Mindful, and Notice

*Awareness is all about restoring your freedom to choose what
you want instead of what your past imposes on you.*
– Deepak Chopra

Be careful how you are talking to yourself because you are listening.
– Lisa M. Hayes

How often do we think about the air that we breathe? It is something we take for granted. Our bodies are on automatic to breathe until someone covers our mouth and nose and all of a sudden our breathing is blocked. Then breathing becomes our number one thought. We are acutely aware of the lack of air.

What we are not so aware of is noticing our thoughts. Through the 13 positive self-talk strategies we will learn how to deepen your awareness and shift to a productive, healthy way of thinking. Here, this second strategy is to be aware.

In every coaching session I ask my clients what they notice about themselves. Asking this has the clients look within. The purpose is to help deepen the clients' awareness and self-awareness. What I am asking them to do is pay attention to how they impact others, how others impact them, and to be mindful of their intentions. Most people typically are only focused on themselves, and they only look at life through their own lens. I am asking them to be aware that everyone's perspective is different, and that people see through their own eyes. I want them to try to see another's point of view by looking at the other perspective. It is asking them to avoid going through life on automatic pilot.

There are different concepts to look at when I talk about awareness.

In addition to being aware of yourself, and of others, it is also important to notice where you feel resistance in your body. You see, your mind can tell you anything, but your body will not lie to you.

For example, you have probably heard of the expression, you can cut the tension in the room with a knife. That expression came about because when you enter a room where there is stress or resistance you can literally feel it.

When you are having a discussion with someone and he or she is resistant in any way you literally feel the resistance. Why? Because as I mentioned before, everything on the planet is made up of energy and we feel energy even though we do not see it. Whether it is tension or giddiness, we feel it.

So again, your mind can tell you anything, but your body will not lie. Your body informs you what is going on around you and what is happening internally.

When I feel anxious about something my body signals me with a "kicked in the stomach" feeling. When that used to happen to me, I would try and push that feeling away. Then, I taught myself a few steps to deal with that feeling. Let's face it, body signals happen to everyone. They show up differently in our bodies. Some people get headaches, others may develop tightness in their chest. The point here, again, is to be aware.

Here are a few steps that can help you when you might otherwise go on autopilot.

First, appreciate that you cannot make a change if you are not aware.

Second, experience the feeling. Do not push it away. It is really the pink elephant in the room—it just gets bigger and it is not going away. Do not try to get rid of thoughts even if you are meditating -- you cannot. Relax and watch the thoughts pass.

Finally, take a positive, forward-moving baby step to replace the "yuck" feeling. After time and practice that yuck feeling diminishes.

For me, when I am anxious and I get that kicked in the stomach feeling, I stop what I am doing. I pause, take a breath, and ask myself, *What is going on in my life that is making me feel anxious or stressed right now?* I then think about it and realize what it is, and I take a small action step in a direction that energizes me and does not deplete me. Not too long afterwards the feeling subsides. Those signals are so important. You have to be awake when they appear.

When having a negative thought I picture a STOP sign in my head. I shift my thought and reframe it in a positive way. For example, instead of saying what I do not want, I say what I do want.

Frame: *I do not want to be around negative people.*

Reframe to: *I only want to be* with *positive people.*

Other ways to increase your awareness are through meditation, mindfulness (putting your attention on your intention), writing down key plans and priorities, and getting feedback from trusted friends or co-workers.

EXERCISE:

Two great apps for meditation, stress reduction, deepening awareness:

www.headspace.com and www.calm.com

BOOK SUGGESTION:

Mindfulness for Beginners by Jon Kabat-Zinn

CHAPTER 3

Strategy 3 - Be Present and In the Moment

Realize deeply that the present moment is all you ever have. Make the Now the primary focus of your life.
– Eckhart Tolle

It is through gratitude for the present moment that the spiritual dimension of life opens up.
– Eckhart Tolle

Being present allows you to live your best life.

Be engaged in what you do. Our brains are wired to take us to the past and the future. Therefore we have to work on bringing ourselves back to the present.

Here are a few tips:

When you hear yourself using the words *could've, should've, or would've,* these are alerts that you are in the past and coming from a place of regret. You were wishing you had done things differently. Thinking in that direction will not serve you. Shift your thinking to what you want to make happen now.

When you hear yourself thinking or saying *what if,* you are in the future and it typically sounds like, *What if this happens or what if that happens.* This thinking can create anxiety.

The key is to get back to the present moment.

I believe that thinking in the present is valuable. That is not to say that thinking in the past or future is not. You just do not want to hang out there. You want to bring your thinking to the here and now.

I recently gave a workshop and asked the group, *What were you thinking when you were in the shower this morning?* Out of thirty people, not one person mentioned anything about the shower. Some responses were, *I have to carpool after work today; I have a meeting at 10:00 and a call at 2:00; I have to pick up the clothes at the dry cleaner; I can't wait to play tennis later.*

Everyone was thinking, but they were not in the present. My advice is no matter what you have going on, focus on what you are doing at the present moment. If your mind wanders, and it will, bring it back into the present moment. Initially you may have to do that a lot. Do not worry about how many times. The important thing is to keep bringing yourself back to the present to create a new healthy habit. In other words, when you are in the kitchen and you are stirring the pot, stir the pot; when you are in the shower, feel the water, notice the lather from the shampoo. Being present is life changing.

Multi-tasking is a process that takes us away from being present. The challenging part is that we do have responsibilities that seemingly direct us to do more than one thing at a time, even though our brains are wired to do one task at a time, we are expected to multitask. So instead of putting our full attention and focus on the task at hand, we typically look at several things at once. We then scratch the surface of many things and do them less than optimally. It is, of course, desirable to focus on one activity and do it well.

I have a client who had an accident. She was multitasking on the treadmill. She explained, *I knew I had several things I needed to do and also wanted to get in exercise.* She added, *I began reading and editing a report I was working on, lost my concentration, and went right off. I was lucky not to have gotten hurt worse … I learned my lesson!*

When you are present and in the moment you are on top of things. You are alive, clear, on time, focused, engaged, and intentional.

EXERCISE:

The following is an exercise involving food that you can do alone, with another person, or with a group. It teaches you to be present and in the moment.

There is no speaking during this exercise. This way you can focus on tasting the foods. Often when people sit down for a meal, they typically are talking to one another, lost in thought, and not focused on what they are eating.

Gather several different types of foods to taste: sour, sweet, salty, spicy, textured, and crunchy.

I typically use lemon, chocolate, wasabi peas, gummy bears, pop rocks, raisins, pickles ... choose whatever you like.

- One at a time, taste each piece of food.
- Roll it around in your mouth (the roof, your tongue, the bottom of your mouth).
- Feel the texture.
- Listen to the sounds.
- Smell the smells.

Is it chewy? Is it crunchy? Soft? Sour? Sweet?

This is an exercise where you are really engaged. Your focus is present and in the moment. You are using all your senses. Enjoy, it's fun!

BOOK SUGGESTION:

The Power of Now by Eckhart Tolle

CHAPTER 4

Strategy 4 - De-Clutter Your Inner and Outer Environment

Inaction breeds doubt and fear. Action breeds confidence and courage. If you want to conquer fear, do not sit home and think about it. Get busy.
— Dale Carnegie

Clutter is not just physical stuff. It's old ideas, toxic relationships and bad habits. Clutter is anything that does not support your better self.
— Eleanor Brown

Clutter isn't just the stuff on the floor. It's anything that gets between you and the life you want to be living.
— Peter Walsh

When I get to the clutter part in one of my workshops I ask, *So who here has clutter?* The general response is a chuckle and almost everyone in the room raises his or her hand; some actually raise two hands!

Most people think of clutter as piles of paper, magazines, newspaper, outdated clothing or clothes in the closet that they never wear.

Clutter is negative energy. It has a heavy, lethargic, bogged down feeling. You get a "stuck" feeling from it. Overwhelm seeps in. Thoughts tend to be in the past.

Clutter comes in three forms:

1.   Physical

2.   Electronic

3.   Emotional

PHYSICAL CLUTTER

Do you have anything that is taking up room in a closet or drawer?

- piles of papers of any kind

- prescriptions in the medicine cabinet that have expired

- outdated food in the refrigerator or pantry

- clothes you have not worn for over one year (which probably are out of style and you are waiting for them to come back in style)

- clothes that you bought and never wore

De-cluttering actually makes us feel better. I have had clients describe that they feel lighter, less burdened. One client said that de-cluttering actually made her feel like bricks were being taken off her shoulders. Another client said he felt like his head was swirling. *I was at the office and took some time to clear my desk, drawers, and I felt like I had more clarity.* He excitedly added, *Next week it's the file cabinet! This is great … I was able to be more productive!*

De-cluttering makes you feel better. Do not think of the process as punishing yourself – have fun with it! Turn on music or the television. Start small with a kitchen drawer, night table, or medicine cabinet. Clearing frees up the energy in your home or office and releases new vitality in your body, your attitude, and your environment. Break de-cluttering into short time intervals if that helps. 'Chunk it down' into timeframes that are reasonable with your schedule. Make it fun! Think of the outcome it will produce. You are getting rid of things that are taking up room and blocking the space for better things. Get rid of what is not working for you anymore so you will have room for what you want.

ELECTRONIC CLUTTER

What does your inbox look like? Are there emails sitting there that you have not deleted or responded to yet? Well, have at it! You will feel better physically and mentally. Again, you do not have to de-clutter all at once. Try ten minutes a day. If you feel like doing more, great!

EMOTIONAL CLUTTER

I view negative self-talk, worry, loose ends, gossip, and drama as emotional clutter. There is usually chaos connected with gossip and drama. As well, loose ends can happen when there are open-ended and unresolved conversations. These are all negatives that take you away from what you want. They deplete rather than energize. Release negative thoughts so that you can fill your mind with productive, useful thoughts. Positively shifting your mindset will produce the results you want.

When you are de-cluttering, if you are not sure whether to throw something away, ask yourself:

- What am I holding onto? Many times the answer is memories or clothes. Interestingly enough, the memories are not always happy and the clothes usually do not come back in style.

- Does this lift my energy and make me feel good or not?

- Figure out if it energizes or depletes you.

- Do I love it and will I use it in the near future?

The following is an energy chart you may find useful:

ENERGY	
Positive	Negative
Flowing, Open Space	Blocks the Space
Positive Self-Talk	Negative Self-Talk
Affirmations	Criticism
Anything that takes you toward your goals, dreams, wants	Anthing that takes you away from your goals, dreams, wants
Connection	Disconnect
Positive Self-Worth	Negative Self-Worth
High Energy	Low Energy
Good Relationships	Bad Relationships

CLUTTER	
Mental	Physical
Negative Thoughts	Piles of Paper
Complaints	Mail
Criticism	Old Clothes
Lack Clarity & Focus	
Loose-ends/ Open-ended Talks	

DE-CLUTTER EXERCISE - TAKE THE CHALLENGE

De-clutter for 15 minutes each day. Start with something small like a desk or kitchen drawer, medicine cabinet, or night table. This is not punitive. You can make it enjoyable. Put on some music or the television. You will begin to have more clarity and focus as you de-clutter and get rid of the heavy, stuck energy. Go to it!

CHAPTER 5

Strategy 5 – Set Healthy Boundaries and Limits

When you say "yes" to others you are actually saying "no" to yourself. This is because the time has to come from something you are doing, whether it's personal time or work time.
— Susan Commander Samakow

I encourage people to remember that "No" is a complete sentence.
— Gavin DeBecker

Whether I am in an individual coaching session or workshop I ask, *How are you at saying "no" when you want to say "no" and "yes" when you want to say "yes"?*

Typically the response is that people say *yes* when they want to say *no*. There are many reasons that people are hesitant about saying *no*.

- They want to be seen as the "nice guy"

- They are uncomfortable saying *no*

- They are pleasers

- They do not know their own limits -- what they will or will not tolerate

Know who you are and what you stand for. Identifying your values is highly important, even key, because your values are who you are at your core. When you know your values you are comfortable with either answer. Knowing your values will help you identify your limits.

Say what you mean and mean what you say. That is what I consider "being in integrity." Integrity happens when what you say and what you do are in alignment.

CONSIDER:

Do your words and actions match?

- If you are trying to lose weight or be healthier, what foods and drinks are you saying *yes* or *no* to? What about exercise? *Yes* for exercising three times per week and *no* for six days per week?
- Is what you are being asked something you can tolerate or a deal breaker?
- Does what you are being asked make you stressed and uncomfortable? (I don't mean being afraid to step out of your comfort zone. I mean not listening to your gut instinct).

CHALLENGE:

For the next three requests, say "no."

COMPLIMENTARY TOOL:

Contact me for a complimentary *Limits & Boundaries* worksheet at susan@selftalkcoach.com.

CHAPTER 6

Strategy 6 – Look at Different Perspectives

When you change the way you look at things
the things you look at change.
– Max Planck

We believe our thoughts are our own. We do not, however, typically stop and think where our perspectives are rooted.

To a large degree, our view of things came from our early years, when influence came from the adults in our lives. Our parents, teachers, religious figures, even our extended families had a very large influence upon us. As we grew up our perspectives broadened and included our peers, other cultures, our education system, organizations, and more. Without realizing it, our perspectives are naturally biased.

Keeping that in mind, when you make a decision, look at it through your perspective as well as other perspectives. Next, weigh out the costs and benefits, or pros and cons of each perspective. It helps to write it all down. Looking at varying views in black and white can help you think of other responses. To take it a step further, particularly when there is an important decision, live in another perspective for a week or two. Try to make decisions from another perspective. See if that works for you. If not, try still another perspective.

Sit quietly for a moment. Think of a situation in your life. Nothing around you has changed except for the way you look at the situation. What shifted? What changed so that your perspective is different?

The next time you have a decision to make:

- Look at it from different perspectives

- Make a list of the possible perspectives

- Next make a list of the pros and cons or benefits and costs and weigh them out

- Choose a perspective and live in it for one to two weeks

- Make all your decisions from that perspective and ask yourself, *Does this feel right? Is this a healthy decision? Am I making my decisions from a place that is best for me (and others involved)?*
  If the answer is yes, then live in that perspective.
  If the answer is no, then try another view and repeat the process.

Here is an example of perspectives for a typical question:

SHOULD I TAKE THIS VACATION?

BENEFITS	COSTS
I need a break	Too much money to spend
Time to recharge	Come back to more work
I'll delegate my work	Co-workers upset with me
I'll be more creative	
I'll be more productive	

CHAPTER 7

Strategy 7 – Choose the Words You Think and Say

Words are powerful. They have the ability to create
a moment and the strength to destroy it.
– Anonymous

Words have the ability to build us up and to tear us down.
Use words to restore us rather than destroy us.
– Dr. Tal Ben-Shahar

I am sure you can all recall, probably in detail, when someone said something that negatively impacted you and it stayed with you for a while, maybe for a lifetime. Be careful how you choose your words. Speak with intention and integrity.

Words, when spoken out loud, transform into vibrations that can be used to direct energy. It is the intention behind the words that conveys the vibration. We want to watch the tone and body language that go along with the words. When I think of the words I choose to say, or listen to the words of others, I think of negative words as junk food and positive words as a good nutritional source. We have to be as careful with the words we choose as we do with what we put into our bodies.

Subtle differences in word choices also reflect positive or negative energy. A few examples:

Would've, could've, and *should've,* as mentioned earlier, reflect past thinking and regret, indicating we wish we had done something differently.

Have to vs. *want to* trigger different energies. The energy of *have to* is desperate and the energy of *want to* comes from desire.

But vs. *yes and* also reflect energies that are vastly opposite. *But* sets up a negative "waiting for the shoe to drop." On the other hand, when *yes and* is used, it communicates acknowledgment and curiosity.

SUGGESTION:

If you are interested in seeing how emotions are calibrated, look at the Levels of Consciousness in Dr. David Hawkins book called *Power vs. Force.*

TIP:

Start noticing when you hear yourself or someone else say: *could've, should've or would've; have to; and but.*

By noticing, you are deepening your awareness. As soon as you notice, shift your language to something positive.

CHAPTER 8

Strategy 8 - Replace and Reframe Negative Self-Talk with Positive Self-Talk

You think 60,000 thoughts a day. Don't waste 59,999
of them on negative, limiting thinking.
– Anonymous

It's not who you are that holds you back, it's who you think you're not.
– Anonymous

Too often we blurt out our thoughts. We want to be aware of what we are thinking and then saying. If we think something negative, pause and consider what we might then say. Replace a negative statement with a positive statement.

For example, instead of saying, *I struck out again*, reframe and replace it with, *Now I know what to do next time*. The key is to say what you do want rather than reinforcing the negative in your neural pathways. Why? Remember, repetition creates and reinforces, and it is to your advantage to create the positive.

SUGGESTION:

On one side of an index card write an example of a negative self-talk phrase; flip the card over and rephrase it to a positive. Use it as a bookmark or keep it in a place as a reminder of *who you were* to *who you are.*

CHAPTER 9

Strategy 9 – Focus on What You Have

When you focus on problems, you'll have more problems. When you focus on possibilities, you'll have more opportunities.
– Anonymous

Each day, focus your attention on what you want. Each day, take one step closer to it. All things are possible. The key is to identify it, claim it for yourself, and believe that you are worthy to have it.
– Iyanla Vanzant

Typically when I get to Strategy 9 in a workshop, I ask participants, *What do you think people focus on?* They usually answer correctly. People tend to focus on what they do not have rather than what they do have. So what do you think they get more of with that type of thinking? Correct, they get more of what they do not want, like a self-fulfilling prophecy.

With a shift in thinking you can focus more on what you do have, because you will then get more of that. And I do not mean by magic.

Once again, thoughts get reinforced in those neural pathways. By shifting our thoughts to positive, productive thoughts, we are reinforcing those neural pathways in our brain. Each time we think positively we are raising our vibration, our level of consciousness or awareness.

When you shift your way of thinking, you change your brain at a cellular level. When you do this consistently, your life changes in the direction of that thinking. If it is positive, you will move in the direction of what you want in your life. You will be energized instead of depleted.

Focusing on what we have, and on what we are grateful for, are positives and true blessings, no matter how large or small. What we think, together with action, is what happens in the world. What we focus on becomes our reality.

Dr. Tal Ben-Shahar is a well-known author and lecturer on Positive Pyschology. In his course, he teaches, *Are you a benefit finder (those who find the positive to focus on and are optimistic) or faultfinder? Benefit finders find the positive to focus on and are optimistic. Do you look at the stars each night or take them for granted? Do you appreciate your family, your work, or your every day? Do you take people, your health, and life for granted or celebrate them? Are you embracing life or living by avoiding it? Do you see stumbling blocks or stepping-stones?*

SUGGESTION:

Here is one way I shift my thoughts that may be helpful to you. I visualize two houses standing in front of me. I call one house the *House of Satisfaction* and the other house the *House of Disappointment.* When I have a negative thought, as soon as I am aware of it, I see the houses and ask myself, *Which house do I want to hang out in?* I then reframe my thoughts to the productive, to the house of satisfaction.

INQUIRIES:

Are you a benefit finder or a faultfinder?

What do you choose to focus on?

CHAPTER 10

Strategy 10 – Realize You Always Have a Choice

We live our life choice by choice by choice.
Freedom is realizing you have a choice.
– T.F. Hodge

May your choices reflect your hopes, not your fears.
– Nelson Mandela

No matter what the circumstances, you always have a choice. This is HUGE. It may not always feel that way, but you do! It is empowering to know this and to take action from this mindset. YOU ALWAYS HAVE A CHOICE. Mindset means choice. Even knowing that has me sit up higher in my chair.

How you feel shows up in your body, in your posture, in your very being. It has you sit up and say, *I am proactive in my thoughts and making choices that empower me.* Use these words as your mantra.

So many people think this is the way it has always been and therefore believe it will continue that way. This is not true. The past is not always representative of the future. You have a choice, so make the choice that is best for you.

Send back to the universe all of the energy that does not help you, and call back the energy that does. Call back all of the energy that is clear, healthy, productive, positive, enriching and loving.

I do an exercise every day, and it involves using my arms and hands. A pushing motion sends back negative energy, and I then pull in that which is positive, that which is mine.

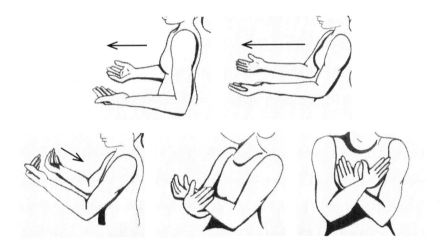

It is okay to have fears. Do not let fears drive your decisions. Make your choices from a survivor mindset and not from a victim mindset. Move your decisions from an unhealed fear to a space that is healed. Be awake to your courage and tenacity. You were born to be happy. That is part of your birthright. Claim it! Claim it now!

EXERCISE:

Send back to the universe all energy that does not belong to you and call back all energy that is yours. Call back your energy that is clear, healthy, and that is beneficial.

Use this mantra daily:

I am sending back all energy that isn't mine.

I am calling back all energy that is mine. My energy is clear, healthy, and benefits me.

SUGGESTION:

When a situation presents itself and you think that you do not have a choice, shift your perspective to, *I always have a choice.* Next, take a step in the direction of choice.

CHAPTER 11

Strategy 11 – Build More Resilience

I am not what happened to me. I am what I choose to become.
– Carl Gustav Jung

Resilient people immediately look at the problem and say,
What's the solution? What is this trying to teach me?
– Anonymous

When life puts you in tough situations don't
say 'why me' instead say, 'try me.'
– Anonymous

Mentioned earlier, resilience is a thinking style and we use that style to deal with adversity in our lives.

Resilience is about mindset. It is about surrounding ourselves with people and situations that energize us and which do not deplete our energy. It is about putting behind what is not working to creating what we do want. It is about taking command of our lives and being proactive, and not reactive. It is about leaving toxic relationships and being in healthy relationships.

I honestly get the chills when I think about all of that. How powerful! You can create what you desire.

When situations with adversity arise, check in with yourself. This is also a way of deepening your awareness. I check in with myself from head to toe, and I check my physical environment. I check my mindset, my energy, and anything I am feeling physically.

INQUIRIES:

How resilient are you?

How do you handle things in your life that have not worked out?

CHAPTER 12

Strategy 12 - Create Your Vision

Never be afraid to try something new. Remember amateurs built the Ark, professionals built the Titanic.
– Anonymous

Create the highest, grandest vision possible for your life because you become what you believe.
– Oprah Winfrey

How do you go about creating a vision for yourself? What works for me is closing my eyes, because there are fewer distractions, and sitting quietly in a place where I cannot be disturbed. No technology allowed! I think about what I want to make happen and then I see it happening. The more details I envision, the better.

SUGGESTIONS:

There are different ways to create your vision. Carve out some time to envision what you would like to create. I recommend a place where you will have privacy and no technology. Being outside is a good way to clear your head before you begin. Take a walk or sit on a bench.

There is no right or wrong, or good or bad way to do this. No judgment. This is a place to start to gain some clarity on what you would like in your life.

Put a stake in the ground and take a stand to create something towards which you can work. You do not have to have the answer right now, and things may change as you move forward, so get started!

Make a list of what you would like in your life and only put on it what you desire, not what you do not want. You can also plan a strategy, use a timeline, and look at the big picture and the details. Anything is possible! It is up to you.

Use a pad, flipchart or whiteboard to draw your vision. You can make stick figures ... you do not have to be an artist.

If you have trouble starting, think of your values and what is important to you. What matters to you? What is your *why*? Focus on the different areas in your life such as health, finance, relationship, career, and spirituality. Think of what you would like to accomplish and then bring your resources and motivation forward to do so.

TIP:

- Be aware of your emotions and the mood you are in when creating your vision. Think of the people you want in your life, the places you want to be, what gives you joy, where you could be of service to others, and so on.

- Ask yourself what legacy do you want to leave? Rather than waiting until the end of your life or career, think in terms of legacy so that you can plan the steps to assure it happens.

CHAPTER 13

Strategy 13 – Practice Gratitude

Be thankful for what you have; you'll end up having more. If you concentrate on what you don't have, you will never, ever have enough.
– Oprah Winfrey

Gratitude opens the door to the power, the creativity, and the wisdom of the universe. You open the door through gratitude.
– Deepak Chopra

Trade your expectations for appreciation and your whole world changes in an instant.
– Tony Robbins

Gratitude is one of the highest vibrations on the planet.

A vibration is a level of consciousness. Consciousness is the state of being awake and being aware of our surroundings. To make any change, we must first be aware.

There are many benefits to practicing gratitude. When you regularly practice gratitude and take the time to notice and reflect on what you are grateful for, you will experience more positive emotions, express more compassion and kindness, strengthen your immune system, and sleep better.

Gratitude is linked to optimism, increased energy, and empathy. It can improve your health, relationships, emotions, career, and personality. When you practice gratitude you are literally changing your brain at a cellular level.

SUGGESTIONS:

Buy a notebook or journal that will be your gratitude journal. Each morning and evening, write six blessings for which you are grateful. It is a wonderful way to begin and end your day. Be consistent so you are able to form a new habit.

Begin to notice or be aware of new things you are grateful for each day. This exercise will improve your life, cultivate an attitude of gratitude, and increase your well-being and happiness. Now that is a positive impact!

In a 2011 study, researchers Cichy and Peters found that the simple writing and delivering of a thank-you letter to someone resulted in both the writer and the recipient enjoying increased happiness levels. Both were seen, by this simple act, to have dramatically improved life satisfaction, which was still impacted weeks later.

Conclusion

It's the repetition of affirmations that leads to belief. And once that belief becomes a deep conviction, things begin to happen.
– Muhammad Ali

EMPOWER, ENGAGE, RESPECT

No matter what relationship or situation you are in, make sure you are engaged, empowered, and respected. Putting yourself in relationships or situations that are disempowering, disrespectful, or disengaging is unacceptable. Respect is your ticket to freedom. When you are heading in this direction you will be following a healthy, positive, forward moving path.

We control our thoughts. They do not control us! Every thought either takes us toward our truth or creates a distance from it.

Be AWARE of what you are saying to yourself and what your resilience level is. Are you critical of yourself? Do you feel drained or energized?

Do a quick check-in with yourself -- on a scale of 1-10, what's your resilience level right now?

Do you put everyone's needs in front of your own? Take great care of yourself. Remember the emergency instructions on an airplane ... put your oxygen mask on first or you will not be able to help anyone else!

Relationship begins with self!

When you practice Positive Self-Talk and Resilience you will lead the life you are meant to live. Use this formula and thrive!

POSITIVE SELF-TALK + RESILIENCE = THRIVING LIFE!

Made in the USA
Middletown, DE
02 September 2018